MW00748018

MAY 2 8 2015

)023

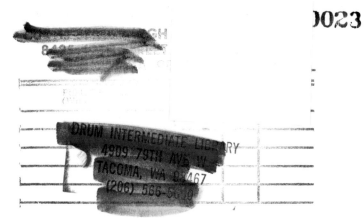

Staying Safe on Public Transportation

Using public transportation presents its own safety hazards.

THE GET PREPARED LIBRARY
VIOLENCE PREVENTION FOR YOUNG WOMEN

Staying Safe on Public Transportation

Donna Chaiet

THE ROSEN PUBLISHING GROUP, INC.
NEW YORK

The author makes no representations or warranties, actual or implied, as to the effectiveness or appropriateness of verbal or physical techniques because it is impossible to predict the variables in any given situation. The use of physical force in self-defense is a response option only when your life is in imminent danger and risk of physical injury is present. The laws regarding use of physical force in self-defense vary from locality to locality, state to state, and country to country, and the techniques described in this book may not conform to your locality's legal standard. In order to best learn and understand the techniques described in this book, "hands on" training and practice are necessary.

Published in 1995 by The Rosen Publishing Group, Inc.
29 East 21st Street, New York, NY 10010

Copyright 1995 by The Rosen Publishing Group, Inc.

First Edition

Manufactured in the United States of America.

Library of Congress Cataloging-in-Publication Data
Chaiet, Donna.
    Staying safe on public transportation / Donna Chaiet. — 1st ed.
      p. cm. — (The get prepared library of violence prevention for young women)
    Includes bibliographical references and index.
    Summary: Uses real-life examples to illustrate how to develop techniques to protect your own safety while traveling alone on various kinds of public transportation.
    ISBN 0-8239-1866-1
    1. Young women—Crimes against—Prevention—Juvenile literature.   2. Violent crimes—Prevention—Juvenile literature.
3. Transportation—Safety measures—Juvenile literature.
4. Local transit crime—Prevention—Juvenile literature.
[1. Teenage girls—Crimes against. 2. Crime prevention.
3. Self-defense. 4. Safety.] I. Title. II. Series: Chaiet, Donna.
Get prepared library of violence prevention for young women.
HV6250.4.W65C526   1995
613.6'0835'2—dc20   95-8476
                                                CIP
                                                  AC

Contents

Introduction

Riding buses and trains presents unique safety problems. Unlike being *at* home, *at* school, or *at* work, taking public transportation invariably means moving around—getting from point A to point B. This often means that you are in an unfamiliar environment and that environment is constantly changing. For example, new passengers get on and off the bus or train, and you may be traveling through neighborhoods where the culture, language, and reference points are different.

Skills that will keep you safe while traveling on public transportation are accessible to everyone. Whether you live in a

city and take public transportation every-
where you go or live in a rural setting and
take buses only to and from school, you
can benefit from good safety habits and
skills. Some of you may be thinking that
since you don't take the New York City
subway you are blessed with perfect safety.
The reality is that crime and violence occur
in many different settings and in many different ways. Most of the safety concepts in
this book work just as well on public transportation as they do if you are hiking.

Taking charge of your personal safety
and learning how to be more self-reliant are
themes developed in this book. Most of you
probably know that it is safest to travel in
groups. You also probably know that if you
feel you are in danger you should try to
reach a "safe haven" such as a police or fire
station, a restaurant, a grocery store, or a
friend's house. This book assumes that you
are going to be traveling alone and must
rely on your own safety skills to keep you
from harm.◆

When traveling on public transportation, you are constantly sur-
rounded by different people.

chapter 1

Assessing the Level of Danger

Many of us acknowledge that riding trains, subways, or buses carries potential risk. The very act of riding a train or bus can make us prey to criminals. We may be distracted with other matters such as reading or finding a seat, or we may not be paying attention. In addition, the commuting process in and of itself creates more opportunities for danger because riding public transportation often isolates us from safety.

The nature of riding public transportation is moving around. You leave your home and neighborhood. You generally have to stand on a platform or in a waiting room, bus stop, or terminal until your train or bus arrives. Thereafter, you get on the train or bus, which stops at regular stations. You cannot get off at any time you wish. Finally you arrive at your stop, get off through another platform or waiting area, and proceed to your destination.

Some distinctions can be made between the safety level of buses and trains. Generally speaking, buses are considered safer than trains. Why do you think that is? Buses tend to be more public. The driver can see most of what is going on in the bus, and bus stops are usually near stores or public places. In contrast, trains are less public. They run underground or overhead, requiring you to take stairs or elevators to get to the platform or waiting room. Also there is usually only one conductor for a number of cars.

In addition to the safety concepts developed later, some safety rules are outlined for your use.

Trains

✓ **Using stairs or elevators to get to the train**

When you ride the subway, try to choose the car in which the
conductor is working.

If you need to take stairs to get to the station or platform, look before you proceed. See if anyone is loitering or following you too closely. If the stairwell changes direction, see if there is a mirror that lets you peek around the corner. Take the stairwell that is most used, even if that means walking an extra block. If you take an elevator, don't get into one with only one or two people or if anything makes you feel uncomfortable. Have your token or pass card in your pocket; don't fumble in a purse or bag. Move quickly and decisively through the turnstile or entryway.

✓ **Purchasing tokens or pass cards**

Have your money (preferably exact change) in a pocket. It is not a good idea to have to take out your wallet to get money. It takes your attention off what is going on around you and lets others know that you have more cash. If you are waiting on a line, be sure to look around; criminals know that you are paying for something and that money is out and available. Keep your wallet in your purse or bag, not in your hand where it could be easily seized or knocked away.

✓ **Waiting for the train**

When you get to the platform or waiting room, take a good look around. Does anything feel wrong or make you uncomfortable? If the answer is yes, leave immediately. Select a spot that is easily accessible to a cashier or vendor or is well populated and well lit. Some train stations have off-hours waiting areas that are surveyed by cameras and/or security people. Take advantage of these spots and use them. Stand away from the train tracks. You don't want to fall accidentally or be in a situation where you can't run away if you see something dangerous, because you have cornered yourself. If you believe a crime is in progress or someone needs assistance, call 911 and be specific about what you saw. "My name is Donna. I am calling from the 3rd Avenue train stop and I saw a man in a gray overcoat threatening a man in a blue ski jacket." Be wary of anyone who creates a scene; this is often a pickpocket's way to distract passengers so that his job is easier.

✓ **Riding the train**

Choose the train car with the conductor, and avoid the first and last cars if they are

In general it is safer to travel in groups.

empty. Watch the ebb and flow of traffic, and notice if anyone who gets on looks agitated, upset, or nervous. If you notice such behavior, move to another car or get off the train and wait for the next one. Place yourself so that you are always facing the other passengers. If you are standing, check behind you at every stop to see who gets on and who gets off. This gesture can look perfectly natural, as if you were looking for an empty seat. Don't do your homework or study on the train. If you are reading and concentrating, you won't be giving your full attention to scanning your surroundings.

✓ Leaving the train

Get off with the crowd rather than being the last one. If you are the last one out, be sure to catch up to the group. Stragglers are more vulnerable.

Buses

✓ Waiting at the bus stop

Be aware of your surroundings and who is standing close to you. Put your back to the bus stop wall so you have a good view of what is going on around you. Pay attention to your instincts; if anything makes you uncomfortable, move away from the bus stop as quickly as possible and go to a safe haven.

✓ Riding the bus

Try to ride toward the front of the bus, as close to the driver as possible. Keep your bag on your lap, not on the floor by your feet.

✓ Getting off at your stop

Be sure to get off and proceed to your destination quickly and decisively.

Always examine your situation. How do you commute? Is it by bus or train? Is the waiting platform or bus stop crowded or isolated? Are there any vendors? Try to determine what parts of your commute increase your danger. Many people ask, "What does a potentially dangerous person or situation look like?" Trust your instincts. If something feels wrong, it probably is wrong. The sooner you make a decision to leave the dangerous situation, the better your chances of avoiding it.◆

chapter 2

Avoiding Dangerous Situations

It may sound obvious, but the best way to stay safe is to avoid dangerous situations. The key to avoiding dangerous situations is to be **aware** and **alert**. You may believe that you have finely tuned awareness skills and that your neighborhood and travel route are "safe." Perhaps that is true. But everyone can benefit from learning more and developing better awareness skills. There are many myths about what kinds of situations are dangerous. Some of you may believe that crime exists only in dark alleys in urban settings. The facts are otherwise. For example, sexual assault is usually committed by someone the victim **17**

Try to ride a subway car that is populated.

knows and in a familiar place (like her home). You need to examine every situation as if it held the potential for danger. That doesn't mean becoming paranoid; it means listening to your instincts and paying attention to what is going on. Let's look at a situation where awareness and assessment skills might be necessary.

Emily

Emily attends City High School for the Performing Arts. It is a prestigious school that requires auditioning for admittance. The problem is that the school's neighborhood has a lot of crime and drug problems. Most students take a bus that lets them off right in front of the school, but Emily has to ride the train system to get to school.

When Emily first started classes at Performing Arts, she was nervous about riding the train. After about a month, however, she felt more comfortable and decided it was not as bad as everyone thought. She got into the habit of rehearsing her lines for the play she was performing in during the train ride. The background noise actually helped her concentrate.

One holiday, Emily was commuting to school because she had a rehearsal. She barely noticed that by the time she got to her stop her car was empty except for one other passenger. As she left the train, he came up from behind and pushed her. Emily was knocked off balance, and as she tried to catch herself he grabbed her shoulder bag. The strap broke, the train doors closed, and he had her bag. Fortunately Emily was not hurt, but she did lose her valuables.

Nobody wants to be mugged, and it certainly was not Emily's fault that she was targeted for crime. However, there are some very specific things you can do that make it less likely that you will be selected for crime. Why was Emily targeted? Was there anything she could have done to prevent the crime?

The most important safety rule is to be aware of your surroundings. The error Emily made was that she failed to stay alert.

Let's see how she might have been able to avoid it.

At the beginning, Emily was nervous about her commute to Performing Arts. There is nothing wrong with being nervous or fearful. Those feelings generally let us know that something is wrong or potentially dangerous. Emily was probably nervous because the neighborhood and train stop were known as high crime areas. Emily could have transformed her nervousness into alertness. That is, she could have been constantly sweeping her surroundings visually to assess whether anything significant was going on. This can be done walking to and from the station as well as when riding the train.

A common characteristic of commuter trains is that passengers are continuously getting on and off during the ride. Take a mental inventory of who gets on and off. In Emily's case, she should have realized that her train was virtually empty. The old saying is true: There is safety in numbers. A better strategy is to be in a train with more people. If Emily had noticed that the train was get-

Criminals look for people who look like victims.

ting progressively empty, she could have moved to another car or the car with the conductor. If all the cars were empty or almost empty, she could have doubled her alertness. This is not the time to have your head in a book. This is the time to be alert and aware.

We know that criminals select victims for many reasons. One of the characteristics that make people look like easy targets is that they look unaware. Emily's habit of rehearsing her lines creates a potential safety problem because it lowers her awareness to the environment.

Vanessa

Let's look at an example of how good awareness skills and quick decision-making can keep you safe. Vanessa was waiting for the bus to go to her afternoon job across town. Out of the corner of her eye, Vanessa saw six teenage boys walking toward the bus stop. She saw that one of the boys had a lead pipe in his hands. They all looked agitated, maybe even drunk or stoned. Vanessa momentarily froze. She could barely breathe. The boy with the lead pipe moved to the front of the crowd and began to head toward the bus stop. Vanessa looked around, but no one else seemed to notice what was happening. She knew there was a restaurant across the street. Vanessa decided she had better get out of that situation really fast. She turned and ran to the restaurant.

Vanessa used a sound strategy to stay safe—she ran away. Running is a very good tactic. However, it is important to run to something, rather than just running. Unless Vanessa was on the track team, I doubt she would be able to outrun teenage boys. The concept is to run *to safety*. In this example, running made a lot of sense. Not only was there a safe place to run to, but she noticed what was happening with enough time to get away. Quick thinking and quick feet saved Vanessa from a potential problem.

Vanessa was also confronted by an additional challenge: She first reacted by freezing. This reaction, often called the "freeze response," is a natural reaction to fear or danger. How many of you have felt startled after a surprise, had a sudden intake of breath, and then felt as if you were unable to move? This freeze response has advantages in nature. Deer freeze in the woods when they are being hunted so that bodily movements don't give their presence away. Luckily for deer, their coloring helps them blend into the environment so that they are hard to see. However, people can't blend into the street or sidewalk, so freezing could put you at a disadvantage.

The goal is not to get rid of the freeze response; that is virtually impossible. The goal is to shorten that response so that you

Trust your instincts about potentially dangerous situations.

can move into another natural response called the "fight or flight" syndrome. This is a physical condition in which your body releases adrenaline and other hormones into your bloodstream that can make you very strong and powerful. You may have heard stories of people accomplishing great feats of strength while they were in emergency situations that put them into an adrenalized state. It is a response that essentially prepares your body for fleeing (as Vanessa did) or confronting the situation. Learning to shorten this freeze response, to **25**

Pay attention to your surroundings when you are waiting for a bus or a car service.

move into the adrenalized state, and to be effective in the adrenalized state is something any of you can do with practice. Chapters 5 and 6 discuss what to do if you can't run away and how you can prepare yourself for that kind of danger.

Vanessa was additionally challenged because her problem was a gang of agitated teenage boys, at least one of whom had a weapon. Dealing with gang violence is beyond the scope of this book. However, it is a good rule to avoid gangs of teenage boys and girls. Vanessa was not chicken in the

above example. She was very aware, reacted quickly, and was able to get to safety.

What if Vanessa had not been alert and
able to get out of the potential danger?
Let's say, for example, that before she realized it, the boy with the pipe had confronted the people at the bus stop and said,
"Empty your pockets." This is no time for
heroics. If someone is demanding your
property and he has a weapon, it is wise to
cooperate.

That doesn't mean that you should
whimper, beg, or cry. You still have
choices. You can breathe, deeply and
slowly. This helps diminish the freeze response. Listen carefully to what is being
said, and don't make any sudden movements. Your property is replaceable; you
are not. Fighting over property does not
make sense.◆

People have a comfort zone that lets them know when other
people are too close.

chapter 3

Verbal Self-Defense Strategies

L et's take a look at some other safety strategies that work equally well whether you are riding a bus or train. These strategies are verbal self-defense. The foundation of verbal skills rests on a concept called "boundaries." A boundary is a physical or emotional line that marks or fixes a limit. Most of you can relate to having a physical space bubble around you. If someone entered your bubble it would make you feel uncomfortable. This bubble is called your "comfort zone." For most people in the United States the comfort zone for conversation is about one arm's length. This is close enough to touch the other person, but not so **29**

The more aware of your boundaries you are, the more likely you are to notice when someone violates them.

close that you could kiss without leaning in.

The comfort zone is important because it is a boundary that can help keep you safe. Think of your house as a boundary that keeps you safe. The more aware you are of your comfort zone and your personal boundaries, the more likely you are to notice a "boundary violation." A boundary violation is a situation in which your comfort zone has been invaded.

Rosa

Rosa rides a bus to school every morn-

ing. The bus is often crowded, and she rarely gets a seat. One morning a passenger sat down next to her and began to doze off. As he fell asleep, his head dropped on her shoulder. Rosa was not quite sure what to do. He was touching her body, but it was unintentional. Even so, she did not like it. She squirmed a little, which woke him up momentarily; but no sooner did he lift his head than he dropped it on her shoulder again. Worse, he began to drool.

Rosa is experiencing a boundary violation. Is her safety in jeopardy? Probably not. The point is that her comfort zone is being invaded. What are her options? Rosa could use a concept experts call "target denial." She could simply get up from her seat and move elsewhere. Disengaging from the target range works very well.

What if Rosa could not easily move away because the bus was packed or she was carrying a lot of bags? This is when verbal skills can be used. She could wake the man and say, "Excuse me. You fell asleep and are leaning on my shoulder. Please stop." This should be said with a clear voice and eye contact. Rosa should be polite, but not apologetic; she did not do anything wrong. There is also no need to speak with anger; the man is leaning on her unintentionally.

What if he behaves differently? What if he sits down next to her and gently touches her knee with his hand. He uses no pressure or force, and he is not hurting Rosa. Is Rosa in any physical danger? The answer is maybe. It is possible that the man is just as unconscious about his hand as he was when he was falling asleep. It is also possible that this man is *intentionally testing* Rosa's boundaries. He is testing how aware she is and what her response will be. We have discussed in earlier chapters how criminals target people who are unaware. Criminals are looking for targets who they think will be easy to overwhelm. One way they figure this out is by giving you a little test, sometimes called the "interview." They see how compliant you are when they create a small invasion. This small invasion (called a boundary violation) could be a

People will invade your boundaries if you let them.

touch as in this example, or it could be asking for directions, or for the time.

Being nice or helpful when the circumstances don't call for it makes you look like an easier target. We don't know whether this man was testing Rosa. The best suggestion is to err on the side of caution. Instead of giving him the benefit of the doubt, give it to yourself. What are Rosa's options? She can get up and disengage herself from this man. She can tell him to stop touching her body. She can say, "Take your hand off my knee." This verbal self-defense strategy is directive language. The tone of voice used should be firm, as when you tell a dog to "Sit." Rosa should also be aware of her body language and eye contact. It is very important that she be congruent. Congruence means that each piece of information she gives about herself says the same thing. If she giggled when she spoke, it wouldn't have the same impact. If she looked down or away, it wouldn't have the same impact. If she whispered the sentence, it wouldn't have the same impact. Everything about Rosa should communicate clear, decisive behavior.

You may be thinking that you could never do that. What if I am wrong, what if he thinks I'm scared, what if I hurt his feelings? Very often young women are concerned about enforcing their comfort zone for fear of offending somebody or making the situation worse. It is important to note that we don't make criminals commit crimes against us. If this were a nice guy who accidentally let his hand rest on Rosa's knee, asking him to move his hand would probably end the situation right there. If he is a jerk, he might say something sarcastic like, "I wouldn't want to touch you anyway," or "You are too ugly to touch." This is not the time to debate your looks. Just calmly repeat yourself until the behavior changes or you can disengage.

If this man had intended to harm Rosa, she was in a win/win situation. If he was testing her and she asked him to stop, then she failed the test and he will probably look for a more compliant target. If he decided to continue to touch Rosa, or grabbed her on the bus, she was in a public place with other passengers and could respond accordingly. Crimes tend to escalate; they

Don't be afraid to put physical distance between yourself and
another passenger if you feel uncomfortable.

don't get better. If this man were testing Rosa to see if she was an easy target, she would want to find this out in a full bus where she could attract attention rather than after he followed her out at her stop and she was alone.

Penelope

Penelope was riding a crowded train. She hated being so close to the other passengers, but she was late and could not wait for another one. Penelope felt a hand on her buttocks. She wasn't quite sure what to do. The hand was open and cradling her body. The touch felt purposeful, not like an accidental brush. Penelope could not move away because the train was so crowded, so she decided to turn sideways and see if that made a difference. This is a type of disengagement. But the strategy didn't work, and he continued to touch her buttocks. Penelope knew she was almost at her stop and would be able to get away from him then. Just at that moment, however, the train stopped and the conductor announced that there would be a slight delay.

Penelope decided that she could not wait any longer and chose to use directive language as a verbal self-defense strategy. She said, "Stop touching my butt." She consciously used a firm tone and made sure her body language communicated the same message. She was careful not to smile so that her message would not be interpreted to mean that she was flirting. Instead of removing his hand, the man whispered in her ear that she had a great ass and he wasn't going to stop. What are Penelope's options?

Some people might suggest that Penelope is being too uptight and that this man's behavior is tolerable. He is not hurting her or threatening her. Others disagree. First, Penelope is experiencing a boundary violation and perhaps the crime of assault. It is not okay for someone to touch her without her permission. Penelope did not give this man permission to touch her body. She has a right to be free from this kind of behavior.

Penelope could use another tactic, which

It can be difficult to stick up for yourself when other people make you uncomfortable.

is to create a scene. The perpetrator here is counting on Penelope's behaving as if nothing is happening (denial) or that what is happening is not so bad (rationalization). She could say in a loud and commanding voice, "This man is touching my body! He won't stop!" Very often this strategy is not used because women don't know how to do it, or feel that they shouldn't make a scene. It is too embarrassing; what if you are wrong and he was just deaf? If that is the case, you can always apologize. However, the better solution is to be safe and get his hand off you. The point is to make other people aware of what is happening. Not that you are relying on them to help you, but this kind of touching (or fondling or exposing oneself) is often done quietly and with the hope that it can stay a secret. Once other people know about it, there is incentive for the perpetrator to stop.

Some of you may be thinking, What if he hits her or grabs her harder? She is not provoking him to attack her. This man is responsible for his behavior. Penelope asked him to stop. She has a right to do that. She did not call him names or insult him. She merely asked him to stop. She cannot control his reaction, but more often than not, the man will stop once others know of his actions.◆

chapter 4

Dealing with Violent Situations

*L*eticia was waiting to catch the train home from her after-school job. It was 6:30 p.m., and she had just missed the 6:28 train. The platform was empty. She wasn't feeling well and decided to walk to the end of the platform to get some fresh air. She noticed out of the corner of her eye that there was a man on the platform, but that was nothing unusual and she turned the other way. He came up to her and asked if she was feeling all right. Leticia couldn't describe exactly what she felt, but she knew there was something "funny" about this man. She was alone and was feeling a little uncomfortable. What can Leticia do to maximize her safety?

Even though there is nothing overtly suspicious about this man or what he is asking her, Leticia can still maintain a safe boundary of approximately two arms' length between them. Not only is the distance important, but her attitude and body language are equally important. We know that much communication occurs on a nonverbal level. We know when our friends are angry, sad, or happy without their having to say a word. Similarly, would-be criminals are experts at getting information from you before even asking you a question. This is a testing or interview process, and it is one test you want to be sure to fail.

Leticia should be conscious of her body language. She should have her head up, her shoulders back, and stand up straight. Very subtle changes in body language speak volumes. (If you want to try this out, stand sideways to a mirror and lean a little forward or a little back and see if you can notice whether you look scared or intimidated.) It is important to communicate calm confidence. She should also bring her arms up in front of her body with her palms

Listen to your instincts when your safety is involved.

facing out and take one step back. Her feet should be facing forward and be wide apart with the legs bent at the knee so that she can stand with good balance. This position looks confident and ready, as compared to fidgety or nervous.

Now that Leticia has good body language, she can use a verbal strategy we already know—clear, directive language. She can say, "I feel fine. Leave me alone." If this were someone who only wanted to make sure she was okay, that should end the exchange. Let's say that the guy wanted **43** to talk more. What if he replied, "You seem like a nice girl. Maybe I could buy you a soda?" Leticia can now use another verbal strategy—she can lie. She can say, "I don't want a soda. I am meeting a friend here and we are going to dinner. He will be angry if he sees me talking with a strange man. Leave me alone." Nobody is owed the truth, and Leticia does not have to continue this discussion. If he means Leticia no harm, he will just walk away.

Let's say the guy is not so nice and says, "Shut up! You're coming with me." This kind of language dramatically changes the dynamics of the situation. He is no longer a stranger inquiring about her health; he is threatening to abduct her. Leticia needs to take a stronger stance. She could try to get the attention of somebody else, perhaps another commuter. Letitia should yell exactly what is going on while identifying her attacker, "There is a man in a green coat trying to abduct and attack me. Call 911." If that doesn't work and he tries to get closer to her or reaches for her, she could start yelling, "Get back. Go away." There are no magic words to say. The goal is to use verbal skills to keep him away from you and to let him know that you are not an easy target.

Most success stories end with a good strong verbal strategy. Yelling loudly and setting boundaries are great self-defense strategies and are available to all of you. Think of situations that you may encounter on public transportation, and think of the things you could do or say to maintain your comfort zone and personal safety. This kind of mental readiness is important. A great way to be ready is to practice visually what you would do.◆

chapter 5

Cabs and Car Services

Cabs and car services are not technically public transportation. They are included here because they present safety problems that are not so different from public transportation. The main differences are that you may not have other passengers getting in and out, and you will probably be alone in the car.

If you are using a car service, be sure to call a reputable one. When you get into the car or cab, lock the doors and put your safety belt on. Pay attention to where the driver is going. You don't want to be overcharged. Avoid illegal taxi services. They often do not have a meter or a rate card and can be quite expensive.

Pay attention to where the driver is going when you ride in a cab.

Kendra

Kendra was at a party in Palmdale, the town next to the one where she lives. Her father was able to drop her off, and she was pretty sure she would be able to get a ride back with someone else's parents. Just in case, she had enough money to take a car service. Kendra lost track of the time talking to friends she doesn't get to see in Palmdale, and she ended up missing her ride. She did not panic, but called a car service. They said they would be there in half an hour.

47

Kendra got into the car and gave the driver her address. On the highway, the driver turned north, and Kendra knew he needed to go south. She asked him why he was going in the opposite direction, and he said he had to pick something up; it would only take 15 minutes. Kendra was suspicious but did not want to be rude and said it was okay. The driver took the next exit and drove another 10 minutes to a deserted house. He went inside and came out with a friend who got into the front seat. Kendra got a very bad feeling about what was going on. She did not know these men, and she was lost. She determined that if he did not get her back onto the highway heading home soon, she was going to do something. Kendra paid careful attention to signs, and soon she spotted an all-night grocery store. She told the driver she was really thirsty and wanted to buy a soda. He agreed. She got out of the car, went into the store, and told the owner what was happening. The store owner went outside and told the driver that Kendra wouldn't need his services. She called her parents and told

*them she would be late; then she got an-
other car service to drive her home.*

Was Kendra in danger in the above example? It's hard to say for sure, but her
decision was good because she got home
safely. Cab drivers should not be running
errands or picking up other passengers.
They are hired to take you somewhere.
What did Kendra do that kept her safe?

The first thing she did was to pay attention to what was happening. She noticed
right away that he was driving in the wrong
direction and she addressed the situation
immediately. He lied to her; he wasn't picking something up; he was picking someone
up. Kendra got an uncomfortable "uh-oh"
feeling and trusted it. She created a plan to
evaluate what was happening, saw an open-
ing to get out of the situation, took it and
made sure she got home safely.

What else could Kendra have done? She
might have tried verbal self-defense strategies. Using clear directive language, she
could have said, "It is not okay to pick up
other people. My parents are expecting me

Trust your instincts. Evaluate any uncomfortable situation and create a plan to reach safety.

home soon. Take me home right away." As long as the driver *was* heading home, Kendra was probably in minimal danger. What if he had said, "I'm not taking you home"? This is now a dangerous situation. He does not have to be any more explicit than that to show that he is planning a crime, probably a sexual assault. Kendra would need to get out of the car as soon as possible—the next time it stopped at a traffic light, or even while it was moving.

Keep in mind that just getting out of the car in an isolated area with nowhere to run to safety is not as good a plan as getting out where a gas station or convenience store is available. The concept is to run to safety. But suppose the car never passed an intersection or all-night gas station or convenience store, and Kendra was afraid she would get hurt if she got out of a moving car. Dealing with this kind of situation is difficult, but not impossible. Kendra should be looking in the back seat of the car for any object she could use as a weapon, such as a bat, a pipe, or a high-heeled shoe. She should study the best opportunity to use it. It might make sense first to hit the man in the passenger seat. In that way, she would be dealing with one guy, not two. It might make sense to wait until the car stopped and begin a physical response then.

There is no "right" solution to this problem. The concept to be stressed is that if you choose to make a physical response, you need to be ruthless and go 100 percent. Pick up a weapon such as stones or dirt, a garbage-can lid, a knapsack, a bat, or a hot cup of coffee and create a plan to use it. If that fails, create another plan. Unlike in the movies, success stories rarely look pretty and are definitely not choreographed like a Bruce Lee film. Think about target areas on the attacker's body such as his eyes, nose, temple, chin, base of the skull, groin, instep, and shins, and think how you can thrust a weapon or an arm or leg into that target area. This is what self-defense is all about. Choose a weapon, choose a target, and when you choose to make your move, go 100 percent.

Learning how to make assessments and how to access your weaponry is not easily taught in a book. Some people believe that it is not a good idea to fight back. They believe that fighting back serves only to anger your attacker(s), and that women have no fighting chance against men, who have greater upper-body strength. The philosophy of my course, Prepare Self-Defense, is that women can make very effective physical responses to danger, especially when they have good training. Good training includes practicing simple techniques in realistic dynamic scenarios.

If you are interested in taking a self-defense class, look for classes like Prepare that concentrate on teaching women to use fighting techniques designed for women's bodies.

In Prepare we teach all of the avoidance techniques and strategies discussed earlier, plus physical techniques practiced against a padded assailant who recreates common attack scenarios. In this way students get to practice what they would do in verbal and physical role plays using full force to the target areas.

The success stories we have received over the past 20 years tell us that attackers are not looking for a fight (if they wanted that they would have attacked a man), and that after the woman has delivered one technique the attacker usually flees. The most techniques a student of ours has had to use to end an assault was three. One of the reasons our success rate is so high is that we capitalize on women's strength, particularly the strength in their hips and legs. We don't teach a lot of upper-body techniques or martial arts that can take years to learn well. The classes are specifically designed for women (and teens and children) and feature a padded attacker.◆

Conclusion

Staying safe while riding public transportation is not dramatically different from staying safe in any area of your life. Learning to be aware and pay attention to what is going on around you is the most important skill you can have. Identifying dangerous situations and figuring out ways to avoid them is *the best* way to stay safe. If you cannot avoid the dangerous situation or your boundaries are being violated, learning easy ways to address the problem verbally is the next best option. If you feel your life is in danger or you are about to be abducted, know that a physical response is an option and that fighting spirit is more important than fighting technique.♦

Public transportation is very useful once you've learned the skills
you need to keep yourself safe.

Glossary

adrenalized state   See fight/flight syndrome.

assailant   Person who commits a crime.

body language   The way we hold our body and the messages and information that communicates to others.

boundary   The physical distance or emotional limit that surrounds a person.

boundary violation   Event in which a person invades your comfort zone with either physical touching or verbal intimidation or disregard for your emotions.

comfort zone   Your own personal physical boundary.

directive language   Words that clearly state what you want, i.e., Stop, Go away, Leave me alone, Back off.

fight/flight syndrome Biological response in which adrenaline and other hormones are released into the bloodstream, enabling the person to fight or run away.

freeze response Biological response to fear or danger that can paralyze a person.

interview process One of the first steps criminals use to evaluate a victim; sometimes referred to as the testing process.

nonvictim attitude Body language, facial expression, and verbal traits that make you look confident and assured.

safe haven Place where you know you will be able to find safety such as a police station, restaurant, grocery store, or friend's house.

sexual violence Criminal behavior including rape, sexual assault, or violence or threats of violence to force a sexual act.

target denial Paying attention and making sure not to put yourself in a place or position where you are likely to be selected for crime.

victim The target of a crime.

Resource List

General Information

National Organization for Women
1000 16th Street NW
Washington, DC 20036
202-331-0066

Women Plan Toronto
736 Bathurst Street
Toronto, Ontario M5S 2R4
416-588-9751

Information on Crime and Victimization

Crime Victims Counseling
P.O. Box 023003
Brooklyn, NY 11202-0060
718-875-5862

In Canada call 1-800-VICTIMS (1-800-842-8467)

Rape Crisis Centers
(For a nationwide listing of rape crisis centers,
  call the Washington, DC, Rape Crisis Center
  Hotline, 202-333-7273, or check the phone
  book for local information)

Hospital Emergency Room
(Ask for Rape Trauma Center)

Ottawa Sexual Assault Support Centre Hotline
613-234-2266

Toronto Rape Crisis Centre Hotline
416-597-8808

The Police
(For emergencies, dial 911; check the phone
    book for local information)

Information on Self-Defense Training

Impact Personal Safety
19310 Ventura Boulevard
Tarzana, California 91356
818-757-3963

Prepare Self-Defense
25 West 43rd Street
New York, NY 10036
800-442-7273

Woman's Way Self Defense
512 Silver Spring Avenue
Silver Spring, MD 20910

The YWCA
(Check the phone book)

Martial Arts
(Check the phone book under Martial Arts or
    Karate)

In Canada, call Impact Personal Safety at 818-
    757-3963 for references to Canadian self-
    defense programs

For Further Reading

Brownmiller, Susan. *Against Our Will: Men, Women, and Rape,* rev.ed. New York: Bantam Books, 1988.

Caignon and Groves. *Her Wits About Her.* New York: Harper and Row, 1987.

Cooney, Judith. *Coping with Sexual Abuse,* rev.ed. New York: Rosen Publishing Group, 1991.

Cooper, Jeff. *Principles of Personal Safety.* Colorado: Paladin Press; 303-443-7352.

Gilligan, Carol. *In a Different Voice: Psychological Theory and Women's Development.* Cambridge: Harvard University Press, 1982.

Mizell, Louis Jr. *Street Sense for Women; How to Stay Safe in a Violent World.* New York: Berkley Publishing Group, 1993.

Index

Acknowledgments

This book is dedicated to Karen Chasen, the Executive Director at Prepare Self Defense. Without her constant support, editorial eye, and sense of humor, none of these books would have been completed. Many other people have taught me about self-defense and personal safety. Listing them all would take many pages. However, my deepest thanks go to Lisa Gaeta, Director of Impact Personal Safety, Los Angeles. Lastly, I want to thank my parents, who have always taught me to "be aware."

About the Author

Donna Chaiet, a practicing attorney in New York City, is the founder and President of Prepare, Inc. Prepare conducts personal safety programs that teach teenagers the verbal and physical skills required to defend themselves by training them to fight against a padded mock assailant. Ms. Chaiet is a recognized speaker and conducts safety/communication seminars for schools, community organizations, and Fortune 500 companies throughout the United States. Ms. Chaiet's frequent television appearances include CBS, NBC, ABC, WOR, FOX, Lifetime, Fox Cable, and New York 1.

Photo Credits

Cover photo by Michael Brandt; pp. 36, 39 by Yung-Hee Chia; all other photos by Kim Sonsky

Design

Kim Sonsky